THANK YOU

FOR PURCHASING THIS MY FIRST HALLOWEEN HIGH CONTRAST BABY BOOK

SCAN THIS CODE TO SEE OUR BOOKS!

PLEASE DON'T FORGET TO LEAVE US AN HONEST REVIEW AND SHARE WITH US YOUR EXPERIENCE AND HOW CAN WE IMPROVE EVEN MORE.

WHY NOT FOLLOW US ON AMAZON.COM?

COPYRIGHT © 2022 BY

WayOfLife™
PUBLISHING

Why High Contrast Images?

Decades of research show that time spent looking at high contrast images is important for a baby's cognitive development. Until about the fifth month, babies use their eyes as the primary source for information about the world and how it works.

Once your baby's pupils are working and his two eyes start to coordinate, he'll be compelled to look at high contrast images, especially from birth to 14 weeks old.

Boo
The cute ghost

Laffy
The happy pumpkin

Halloween Kettle

Halloween Castle

Flowwy
The flowing ghost

HAPPY
HALLOWEEN

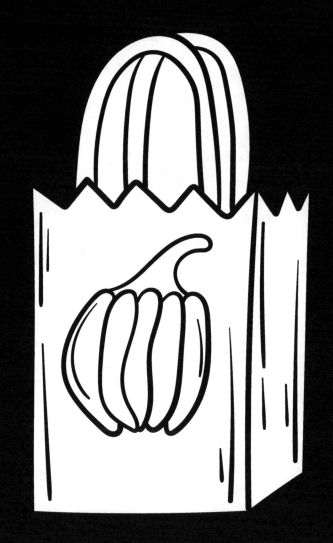

Candy Bag

Carlisen

The flying witch

4 Moods

The pumpkin friends

TRICK OR TREAT

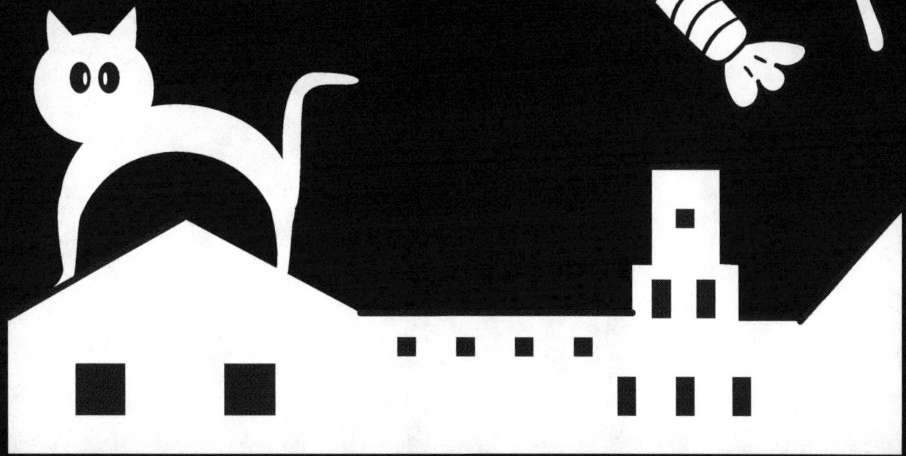

Cake

Losirnal

The original pumpkin

Vampiro
The friendly vampire

Kimsonil

The so cute ghost

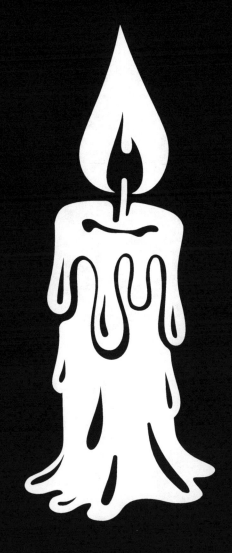

Candle

Moon Bats

Pumandy
The candy pumpkin

Spider Web

Stars Moon

Wir

The jumpy cat

Inno
The innocent ghost

Bati

The explorer bat

Empy
The pumpkin candy bag

Made in the USA
Columbia, SC
19 October 2023

24657046R00015